BAIT BOX STEW

Bets Cottage, Cadgwith

BAIT BOX STEW

Graham Clarke's

CORNWALL

GRAHAM CLARKE

THIRD MILLENNIUM PUBLISHING

First published 2000 by Graham Clarke Limited & Third Millennium Publishing Limited
Shawlands Court, Lingfield, Surrey RH7 6BL

ISBN 0 9536969 2 8

A catalogue record of this book is available from the British Library

Printed in Italy by Valente on Fedrigoni Arcoprint

INTRODUCTION

If it were possible to ask the population of ENGLAND to name their favourite County, I believe Cornwall would be top of the list. Were you to ask the same question in CORNWALL the answer would probably be a gruff "Cornwall 'course are'ee daft or wot?"

The Cornish are proud of their home territory and with every justification.

Cornwall has played a unique part in our history, it retains great respect for the past with a strong sense of mystery, magic and wonder. Cornwall has it's own language and a wild Celtic spirit that while not wishing to offend 'up country' England considers itself a land apart, cross the river Tamar and you're in another country, it certainly feels like it. Cornwall is a Duchy, a Dukedom and has been since Edward the Black Prince was made it's first Duke more than 650 years ago.

Cornwall has been host to millions of happy holiday makers, sent it's famous miners and engineers all over the globe, given us inspiring preachers and poets, fearless sailors, rousing songs, brave fishermen and lovely fish.

As may be inferred from the title this book only deals with aspects and locations that I know best so forgive me if your own favourite spot does not get mentioned.

Apologies too for the spelling errors of which I am informed there are rather a lot, likewise deveations from accepted punctuation I am afraid the rather unusual method of book production used, avoiding the services of editor, designer and gives little oppotunity for correction. typographer

For those readers who can find no mistakes "welcome to the club."

For those who can, but agree that it doesn't matter too much anyway— many thanks.

My dear wife Wendy comes into this second category and I also thank her for the hundred ways in which she ensures that my working hours are not only made possible but are worthwhile and enjoyable as well.

She shares with me in dedicating this book to our very many much loved and respected Cornish friends.

G.C. June 1997

Kynance Cove

CORNWALL first worked its spell upon me rather more than 53 years ago. There was a WAR going on and to avoid the latest spate of buzz bombs and doodlebugs yet again we hastily left our suburban semi in the vulnerable Kentish corner of poor old London and fled to more peaceful surroundings. On this occasion to a tiny slate quarrymans cottage in DELABOLE, NORTH CORNWALL. I was 2½ and brother Tony a couple of years older, very sensibly we took our mum along too. I was told later how very kind Mr & Mrs. Pooley had been to us. Frequently reminding us of how much safer we'd be with them.
"Just let ol' 'Itler come snoopin' round these parts we'll soon show 'im." Mr. Pooley would say. Then to reassure us open the cupboard next to the blazing Cornish range and get out his sticks of dynamite. He'd borrowed them from work of course as had most of his mates.

It was from this cottage that one sunny day, being heavily armed with Mrs. P's pasties we made an expedition to the seaside. For our mother, never a robust walker at the best of times this proved an unforgetably arduous experience, for the steepness of the hills, the combined tonnage of me and the pasties and the uncommonly elastic length of the Cornish 'mile'. I believe it to be the first real memory of my life. For the first time I saw and marvelled at the sea, a gigantic sweep of blue blue water, the first

time I'd ever seen the stuff in such magnificent abundance. It worked its indelible magic and the word "TREBARWITH" brings to the minds eye a great panoramic sweep of sand, sea and sky and just as vividly a fresh salty smell of it all is experienced somewhere inside my head.

Mrs. Pooley it was said, always referred to me as her 'King', very nice too and with King Arthur's Tintagel being only a Cornish mile or three away and my middle name also being Arthur perhaps she forsaw the promised return of the great warrior King in the country's hour of need. On the other hand maybe she called all little boys the same to save learning names. We'll never know.

Trebarwith

Just as we had settled into the cosy warmth provided by the nice Pooleys the juvenile population of the village including us boys came out in red spots; not as bad as green or purple maybe. Bad enough for us to be suddenly trundled off to LAUNCESTON to stay with some incredibly old aunts apparently belonging to my Granny though.

Family legend states that on one particular market day a wayward cow reluctant to come beneath the auctioneers hammer decided to seek refuge through the old aunts front door and had got half way up the narrow staircase before being discovered.

It is tempting to think that if the poor beast had managed to put on a nice lace bonnet and actually get tucked up in bed she might well have got away with it. Funny old things aunts.

Southgate

LAUNCESTON 1997

A very pleasant historic market town, once Cornwalls capital it was disqualified some time ago for being almost in Devon. It reminded me of the fortified hilltop towns in the South of France with its castle, fine church and a remarkable number of establishments calling themselves Bistros.

Bazil Bolitho
Cadgwith

In common with countless other English visitors over the last century or two CORNWALL was the chosen land for several Clarke Family holidays. I must have been ten or eleven when packed in the elderly Wolsely we were juddered from our bit of South East LONDON down to the Belmont Hotel, LOOE.

LOOE I discovered was East LOOE and WEST LOOE with a nice stone bridge connecting the two, I loved it.

Especially the sturdy wooden fishing boats two by two all along the quayside, like fat little Spanish galleons. I drew them, for I was already an artist, a proffessional one too since I readily accepted money for my pictures, ten shillings once from a nice lady up the road, twenty weeks pocket money all in one go.

But I needed to sail a boat; no one would come with me so I took myself to the boating lake, an old tidal millpond up river towards the corrugated iron Pilchard Cannery. I had invested in a little book Sailing for Begginers (cheap) and briefly skipped through it, a bit technical for me. I paid my fee for a single sail craft and drifted aimlessly about the dead calm waters for the alloted 30 mins. It was an adventure alright but not like the catching of the Eel.

Brother Tony desperately needed to go fishing, quite right too of course. The owner of the Belmont a very jolly person with a very long and interesting nose kindly lent us a hand line so we rushed down to have a 'chuck in' below the bridge. To our utter astonishment we caught something, up the thing came slashing and banging about against the slippery black quayside. It was no good hitting him on the head we discovered, in fact he seemed to thrive on it expertly entangling himself amongst a mile or two of Mr. Belmonts fishing line. We wish we'd never caught the monster, he was eventually despatched with the aid of a miniature penknife and a boot a long and grisly job. We reckoned if he'd been chopped up and stewed for an hour he'd still be flying about the dinner plate. But that was not his destiny, we cut the line and threw him back in the murky waters then we sloped miserably back to the hotel, eels were not proper fish we decided, altogether far too snakey for their own good.

This piscatorial dissapointment was pleasantly offset by a young mans dream that did come true, we were allowed to ride on the footplate of a small steam engine. Only 50 yards or so in Looe railway station but never to be forgotten.

14

LOOE 1997

My millpond boating lake had shrunk, most of it now filled in to become a car park. The Belmont Hotel was still there as Belmont Apartments but the town appeared to have sold it's soul to commercialism, most of what was on offer being quite inappropriate to such a place. Plenty of nice fishing boats both new and old and a thriving fish market so that was good.

Took home some cheerful looking red bream or *Pagellus bogaraveo* as they prefer to be called.

As I wandered along the quay the thought struck me yet again that fishermen in harbours like this have had to acquire an ability to carry on a days work while being gawped at snap-shotted and asked daft questions by crowds of people with nothing better to do; worse than being an outdoor artist.

Wendy and I went again to Looe on a warm breezy day in early summer the river was as busy as Venice's GRAND Canal; most satisfactory.

PAGE No. 15

POLPERRO 1950's

From LOOE it was a short but choppy boat trip along the coast to POLPERRO. The gifty shops with their Piskey grottos, the picture book cottages reflected giddily in the little harbour didn't offend my artistic sensibilities, I considered the whole place absolutely marvellous. I purchased a sort frog creature made of several scallop and limpet shells cemented together, with a huge gaping mouth and goggle eyes. I considered it an exellent work of art having seen nothing like it ever before. My parents I recall were not so sure but I think it was a financial rather than aesthetic judgement where they were concerned.

My ten shillings was nearly gone but just enough remained for me to become the owner of a genuine solid brass Cornish Piskey, the label on his packet promised to bring good luck. I am pleased to report that this has proved highly effective over the intervening 47 years and must represent excellent value at one shilling and ninepence. ⇒ HIM

PAGE 16

POLPERRO 1997

At first wondered whether it was a good idea to return to POLPERRO, it had become so intensively commercialised. As I wandered through the village it didn't look so pretty, it was wearing too much make up. though it needed none.

The harbour itself was better with a good fish stall with "en suite" crab boiling facilities and plenty of freshly painted elderly boats.

It's still a nice place Polperro of course and well worth a visit. That's it's problem.

2 very similar winkles

Polperro Harbour

Gweek

A year or two after our marriage Wendy and I had aquired our first car and a nice baby to sit in the back so we set off for the first Cornish family holiday of our very own. We stayed at GWEEK at the top end of the short but very beautiful Helford River. We were in a holiday flat right by the water, owned and meticulously maintained by a most interesting person. He was far too neat and precise to be a Cornishman, this being no insult whatever to either him or them. He was not the retired headmaster of a lesser public school in Surrey, but as we discovered later the former owner of a famous PICKLE & CHUTNEY empire, and very good stuff too. Just goes to show, Eh?

The baby in the car was of course our son Jason, upon our arrival after a long and unpleasanly eventful journey he was duly tucked up in his cot, the welcome peace and tranquility worked it's charm and he was very soon fast asleep.

Then to our astonishment like the most monstrous clap of thunder the GWEEK SILVER BAND struck up the first great blasting oompah of its special rehearsal. A random collection of boys, girls and old men sitting on wooden benches were blasting away a dozen yards across the water. Apparently they had been gently banished from the village centre for their extra practices prior to the forthcoming WEST of ENGLAND brass band competition onto the spur of land below the boatyard opposite Jasons bedroom window. We loved the music, all three of us and recieved a free concert on most evenings of our two week holiday, as a consequence we were able to learn the three or four tunes by heart, very thoroughly indeed.

I think I know what you're trying to say.

GWEEK
We stayed at several times over a period of some years and frequently enjoyed the warmth and generosity of the CORNISH people. Nice Mrs. Thomas from up past the chapel made us fruit cakes and pasties while Mr. Thomas told me to freely make use of his boat. In our daily wanderings for me to make my drawings and play sandcastles we discovered romantic Gunwalloe with its extraordinary little church, Mullion, its fine cove and crab sandwiches, leafy Helford, proud Coverack and most perfect of all wonderful Cadgwith. I dew and painted this special place several times never dreaming that one day we would have a little cottage of our own right there on the beach.

PAGE No.
19

Mullion

About a mile from Mullion village lies the famous Cove with it's miniature harbour. When I was about 12 years old I did an oil painting of this place, I have to admit that I copied from a postcard of someone elses work. I don't think I approved of this kind of expropriation even then but I did so much wish to paint such scenes. It was to be more than a dozen years before I could work from the real thing, I made sketches, paintings, woodcuts and some years later an etching for the National Trust. They own the place and keep a watchful eye open for what needs attending to, particularly after one of the great storms that so often can blast in from the SOUTH WEST. Mullion has it's very own desert island just offshore but it provides only partial protection on such occasions.

On the Southerly Side built tight into the rocks above the harbour wall is a stone hut that must be one of the most photographed buildings in the land humble though it is. It was here years ago that we used to watch old Mister Munday make his crab pots from a stack of willow withes, thinking then that the art must die with him, happily we were wrong, (see page 24.)

A few miles further South, and if you proceed much further you'll be off the end, is KYNANCE COVE with the most spectacular coastal scenery in Cornwall.

Lord Leighton described it thus:— "Perfectly unique; a lovely picture, the finest cove in the kingdom".

I don't know who Lord Leighton was but he was'nt far off the mark. *

* I've looked up this LORD LEIGHTON, in my Little book, he was Frederick, 1ST Baron Leighton of Streton (1830—1896) a famous painter and sculptor, he even sold some bits to Queen Victoria apparently.

"PROPER JOB"

PAGE No. 23

The Harbour, Mullion.

On the way out of MULLION village as you turn the corner to go down to Cove is an impressive reminder of the work of the Royal National Lifeboat Institution, almost a wayside shrine. You can check the correct time on the clock, look at the thermometer, forecast the weather on the venerable barometer and make a donation to this most worthy cause.

The catching of crabs lobsters and crawfish has been going on down in Cornwall since Stone Age times and a baited trap in the form of a cleverly designed wicker pot for many hundreds of years has been the tool of the trade. Nowadays crab pots consist of a metal frame covered with plastic netting and very durable they are too. But at least one fisherman knows how to make them in the old style, he learned from his father, then a few years ago revived the skill to make pots for his own use and handsome souvenirs for the visitors.

Nigel, Cadgwith.

BAIT BOX STEW (THE SONG)

1. Find a Cornish fisherman brave and strong and true,
In his jolly fishing boat red or white or blue,
Suggest it most politely that he might give to you,
A few bits from his bait box for your bait box stew.
A haddock or a halibut a pollack or a dab,
A flounder or an octopus a gurnard or a crab.
But not his precious lobster or he might give to you
A clip around your lug'ole for your bait box stew.

Ch. Bait Box Stew, It is so good for you,
Distemper, croup or fainting fits a broken leg or flu,
Just tap upon my cottage door and try a bowl or two
'Tez 'andsome an' 'tez proper an' 'tez bait box stew.

2. Take your average frenchman with his soppy frenchmans hat,
He likes his grub and glass of wine, maybe that's why he's fat,
He likes his Bait Box Stew as well but with his foreign ways
Doesn't call it Bait Box Stew but bloomin' "Booley Baize"!
A Cornishman in Switzerland got buried in the snow,
And said, "I'd better pray a little prayer before I go"
Then appeared a brandy barrel and a big St. Bernard,
"You can keep your brandy boy, I'ze prayin' for a
                                                    gurnard."

Ch. Bait Box Stew Etc.

(CONTINUED ON NEXT PAGE ➔)

PAGE No. 27

HEARING

HERE

GROUPER?

"PERCY THE P____"

JOHN DORY

NOT A GURNARD ➔

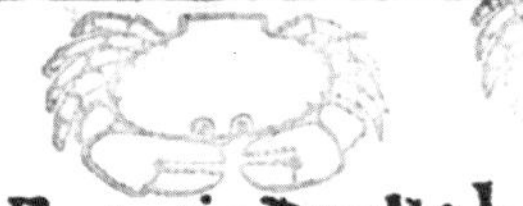

3. Famous Francis Drake boys that sailed the seven seas,
Loved his kippers and custard boys with jellyfish and peas,
When he ran out of powder, now would I lie to you?
'E loaded up his cannon boys with bait box stew.
Admiral Lord Nelson he really loved it too,
He gave it to his captains and he forced it down the crew,
He loved the Lady Hamilton and so the sailors said
She gave him quite a bit of it before he went to bed.

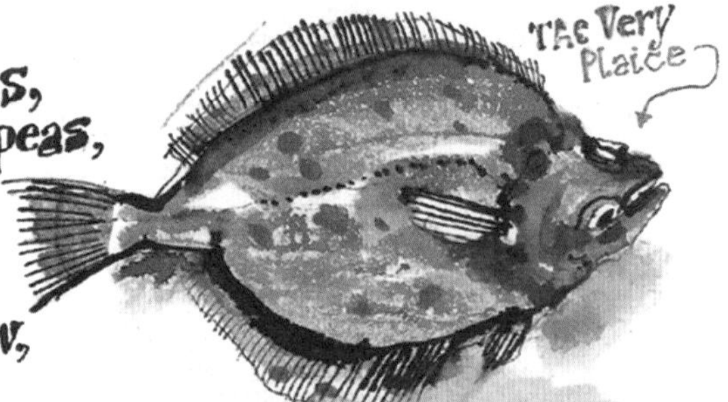

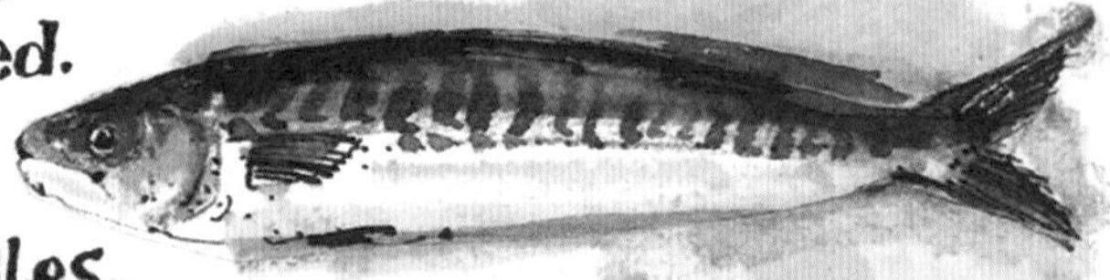

Ch. Bait Box Stew Etc.

4. A charming little Chinaman very fond of noodles,
Of bird's nest soup and puppy dogs, Alsatians, pugs and poodles,
Came down 'ere to CORNWALL with diet rather nasty,
Went to Sharkey's café boys and asked for Seagull pastie!
An ugly little Martian came flyin' out the sky,
Said "how'd you like a nice slice of STARGAZEY PIE?"
Ever so politely we says, "No thank you."
"The reason we're so 'ansome mate is Bait Box Stew."

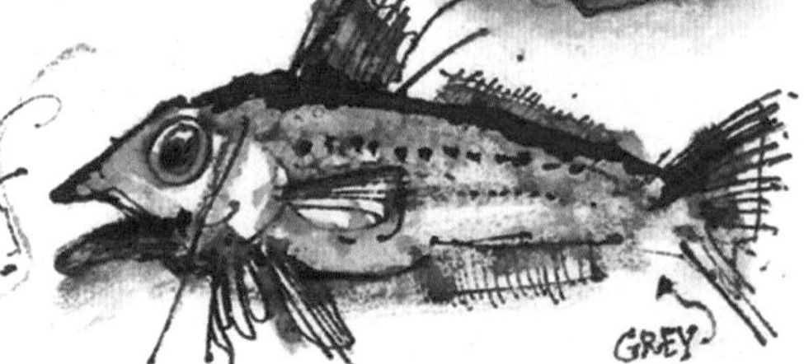

Ch. Bait Box Stew Etc.

P.S. If you're having a party and got to feed a group,
Chuck a bucket of water in and tell 'em it's BAIT BOX SOUP!

'THE very
Plaice

Limpet

GREY
GURNARDS
RED

Cadgwith, Todden Cottage & Steamers House.

GUNWALLOE is a place of mystery and romance which we first discovered when staying at nearby Gweek. The extraordinary church is dedicated to St. Winwalloe and many years ago I made an etching called 'St. Winwalloe's Dream' in which the little cove had become a safe harbour and a nice village had sprung up around the church. His dream (my dream) has yet to materialise.

According to history a notorious buccaneer Captain Emery buried vast quantities of treasure in the sands right by the church wall. You may not believe the story but JOHN KNILL, Collector of Customs at St. Ives did and in 1770 obtained a grant of treasure trove, he searched diligently but found nothing, 'Knill' as you might say. Then a few years later a ship was wrecked here, a common enough occurence but this one had been carrying 2½ Tons of gold coins. For some years every time there was a decent storm money could be picked up from the beach. In 1845 serious efforts were made to sink a 'dollar mine' to speed things up. Build a dam, pump out the water and retrieve the spondulicks with relative ease. Alas a breeze sprung up from the South West and quickly demolished all traces of the venture. Too greedy we might suppose?

Gunwalloe

Grade Church; lonely but loved is this fine structure, it can be seen from many miles around, there was once something of a village up here too so they say but there's little sign of it now.

Uncle Howard who keeps an eye on the roof kindly invited us up the tower one sunny afternoon, it was like upside down potholding so narrow, dusty and dark were the crumbling steps and odd angled hatchways; the view from the top was well worth the effort of course, sunshine never was so bright.

Come to Good, a wonderful name for a most special place of worship. A Friends Meeting House tucked away in the woods south of Truro. The Cornish Quakers built it for themselves in the early 1700's. A barn like structure made with economy and devotion and cared for in the same way today. Inside and outside a perfect example of undecorated rustic elegance.

Come to Good

Whether Jesus really came to Cornwall as a boy with Joseph of Arimethea to trade for tin we can't be sure, some Cornish folk certainly like to believe so and I am much inclined to join them.

Our great poet William Blake must have heard the story and been at least half convinced when he wrote:-

"And did those feet in ancient time walk upon England's mountains green?"

Anyway, the mining of tin and other valuable metals has been carried out in this part of the world for at least 2,000 years and had become a huge industry once steam power had been mastered; by the middle of the nineteenth century there were a thousand engine houses across west Cornwall, many of them remain as gaunt reminders of a more prosperous time. ≫➤

One of the delights of Cornwall and one I suspect that the Cornish rather take for granted is the abundance of small old fashioned independent bakers shops. Offering saffron cakes, leopard loaves, scones to have plastered with too much lovely cream, the famous pasties and proper bread.

All is not lost, with a bit of work done on them they will make excellent castles when the need arises.

* A bun dance ≫➤

Engine Houses, Wheal Peevor Mine.

Today 27th February is my birthday, I am 56 years old a good enough reason to make a pilgrimage. So for the first time since I was but a titchy toddler, away up to see the 'largest hole in the country', Delabole's slate quarry and the grandeur of North Cornwall's finest beach Trebarwith Strand, neither proved dissapointing.

The quarry is indeed gigantic, half a mile across a mile and a half around its irregular perimeter nearly 500 feet deep and getting bigger all the time.

Who knows how many sturdy slate roofs, shining bar tops, elegant floors and dignified tombstones have been hewn from this great chasm over the last 600 years? Not me.

We admired the examples of the numerous uses it can be put to in the showroom including bar tops and dining tables which naturally reminded us of lunch.

Our guide on this outing was Squeeze-Box Dave who for some years was landlord of 'The Port William', a nice pub at and almost on Trebarwith Strand. Obviously this was to be the victualling post for the birthday lunch.

Nothing posh you understand, seafood platter as they call it and chips. The Strand is approached down a long coomb which ends abruptly with a fine view of the sea between great jagged cliffs with the hump of Gull Rock just offshore, It looks more like a giant hamster than a gull but none the less spectacular for that.

It was no surprise to discover later that old King Arthur (a local boy) fought a famous battle here and he couldn't have picked a nicer spot. Whether it was against Saxons, Picts, Irish or simply the usual summer visitors from Croydon history does not reveal.

A POEM

"I remember this marvellous Trebarwith,
When little I went there, my Ma with,
But lanes steep and narrow need bike pram
                                        or barrow,
As there's hardly a yard that's a car width."

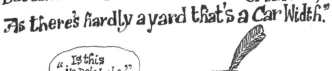

" Is this "in Delabole" ink?"

POETRY INK

Slate Quarry, Delabole.

STORMY WEATHER, severe gales from the South, possible surge tides, winds up to 90mph. That probably means trouble down in the cove. High water is predicted for six o-clock this evening but the biggest most destructive waves can roar in any time an hour or so before or after. The tide table does not indicate a particularly high one, but neither did it prior to the famously awfull storm of three years ago, the one that burst in cottage doorways and effortlessly lifted great chunks of the road. This was was the one that the old folk who normally had 'seen it all before' readily admitted it was "probbly the worse ever."

A neighbourly phone call late in the afternoon suggests I close the storm shutters on our little house down by the beach, I realise I should have done it sooner, so we hurry down the hill. The fishermen have already moved their boats from the hard standing at the head of the beach, dragging them with an old tractor made entirely of rust either up the hill out of harms way or across the road to tuck between the cottages. We close the shutters and secure the seven bolts whos job it is is to keep

at bay the combined forces of the English Channel and Atlantic Ocean. Then join a small group of spectators to marvel at the Wondrous unpredictable powers of nature. These great waves now hurling themselves into the cove, are they 20 feet high 30 feet how many thousand tons of boiling ocean does each one contain?
In an hour's time will the road we are now standing on still be in place? Will our cottage be awash with broken boats, dead fish, boulders and seaweed?
But on this occasion nature was to be kind to Cadgwith, by six o-clock the Southern gales unexpectedly swung around to the West. Not so good for Mullion and Porthleven of course but a welcome enough anticlimax for us.

PAGE No.
38

IF THIS IS SUPPOSED TO BE A MULLET I'M A MONKEY'S UNCLE

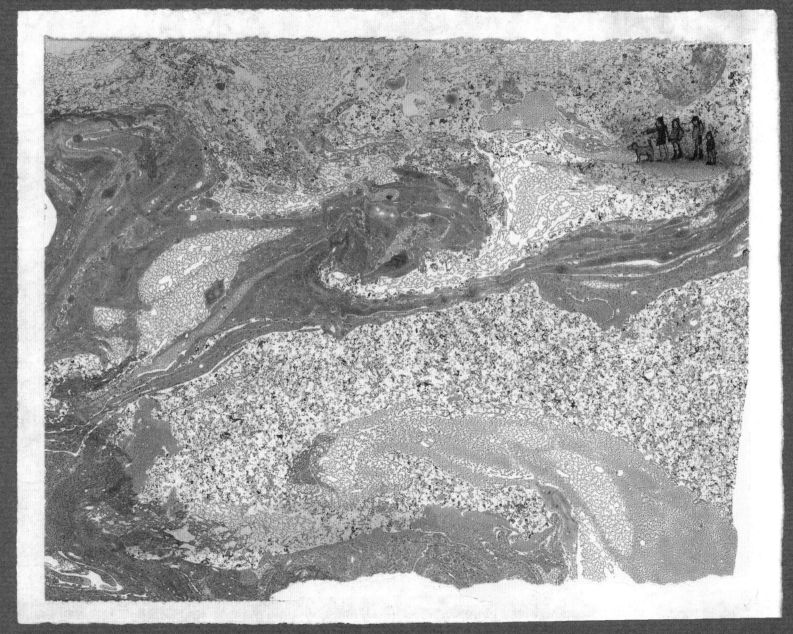

"Twice a day an island" is St. Michael's Mount or to be more precise twice every 24 hours 51 minutes. Each low tide reveals the rough causeway that winds its way across the sands. The causeway is constructed of the most varied lumps of rock you're likely to see outside a geological museum and all the better when still wet and shining from a retreating tide.

This place, small though it maybe was for centuries an International Trading port. Ancient Greeks knew all about it as did old Julius Caesar, it was renowned for the export of valuable Cornish tin.

A Benedictine Priory was built here by Abbot Bernard Le Bec of Mont St. Michel in Normandy in 1135, presumably he was hoping to open a branch office overseas, and so he did.

But it was a holy place centuries before that, what Celtic missionary could have resisted such a site for a nice peaceful little chapel? And what valorous soldier resist such a site to build a fortress? They couldn't and didn't and so it became a castle as well.

Since 1659 it has been the home of the St. Aubyn Family most of whom have been named John it would seem, the present John having produced an excellent History & Guide to his most especial domain.

All the radio weatherman can offer us is more rain with westerly gales at best but I decide to go and look at famous St MICHAEL'S MOUNT again anyway. I might be able to make a drawing from inside my van. Granite milestones painted carefully in black & white mark the way.

Penzance 12 Miles Lands End 22
Penzance 11 Miles Lands End 21
Penzance 10 Miles Lands End 20,

PAGE No. 42

Some have pointing hands or arrows on them too so you can be absolutely certain you're going in the right direction, they serve as a timely reminder to any driver with bad brakes to reduce speed. "You are approaching the edge of the known world."

A few miles short of Penzance I turn down into MARAZION a fine little place especially in the winter (palm trees are ever-green) such a pleasantly exotic medley of pubs, chapels, cafés and cottages. No doubt their builders thought they ought to do "Summat a bit special like", in the face of the architectural grandeur on the noble isle just offshore. I find a place with a good view across to the MOUNT. The tide is out, exposing the rough causeway curving across the sands to the little harbour and neat collection of cottages and stores gathered below the great castle. The tide is out and a few brave souls leaning into the gale struggle over on foot. Grey sheets of rain sweep in from Mounts Bay where great creamy rollers are bowling in hot on each others heels. Suddenly the whole scene all but dissapears, Cornwall's most glorious landmark already the subject of a myriad artistic endevours will have to wait until another day for mine.

Halfway home the foursquare tower of Breage Church reveals itself through the drizzle and today to brighten things up it looks as green as a mouldy penny.

Celtic Cross in Breage Churchyard

St. Michael's Mount on a slightly better day.

St. Michael's Mount, Entrance Gate.

Ruan Minor

One fine Sunday morning in ZENNOR church just as the choir and congregation had completed their shuffling and were beggining to settle down they were joined by a stranger, a beautifull young Lady with green eyes of greenest green.
She was wearing a longdress which was just as well or they might have noticed that she was in fact a mermaid. Don't ask how she was able to transport her personage up from the seaside on her fishy tail, this a legend.
There were some fine singers in the choir but none finer or more handsome than Mathy Trewhella. Young Mathy didn't hear a word of the sermon, he was oth'wise occupied as you might say with a vision of beauty the like of which he had never beheld smiling at him with green eyes from the back pew. He must find out who she was.
Typical of a mermaid, she slipped away half way through the benediction.
This went on for several Sundays until Mathy, being a bright lad nipped out before time himself through a little side door. He was waiting for her out in the sunshine, she seemed to be expecting this, she smiled sweetly and took his arm.
In fact she didn't only take his arm she took the rest of him as well, they took the path down to the green green sea and poor Mrs. Trewhella never saw her lovely boy again.

ever? ever

Zennor

The Late February gales blustering in from the Atlantic seem to have blown themselves away and taken the horizontal driving grey drizzles along with them. It's daybreak; robins and blackbirds just like me are delighted with this improvemt in the weather and sit amongst the bare twigs of the hedgerow passing on the good news.

The sea, a short quarter of a mile down one of the steepest hills in the whole of Cornwall appears a milky green from up here with a few white horses still barging about to the east of Lizard Point. There's not a ship to be seen even though the horizon is as sharp as a carving knife.

The Cadgwith rooks across the valley ratchet and croak, fussing about in their tree tops, at last able to get on with nest building.

Timmy's midnight cat sits huddled on his granite window sill waiting to be let in. Beyond Timmy's farmhouse a few orange cows punctuate the steep grey hillside; a delight to the eye. It's just below here a little further down the hill where careless cows slip right through the rough hedge into the lane. Not very pleasant for the poor beasts but far worse for late night pedestrians still a bit fuzzy from the pub struggling back up the hill.

One of the cottages is having a new ridge to it's thatched roof, despite the weather, the work has gone well; how handfuls of wispy straw can be transformed into such a huge decorative work of art amidst the gales is a wonder indeed.

Round the sharp corner by Bert Wylie's cottage and so down into the cove; sitting in the middle of the road is a very nice little spaniel, a 'King Charles', very much like our Jessy back home in Kent.

Though he dosent remember it I met him six months ago when he first arrived in the village, a tiny puppy in a cardboard box at the back of the Watchouse. I ask his name but it seems he's been instructed not to talk to strangers, I'll find out later.

The fishing boats have names too, right at the top of the beach on account of the weather, 'Razorbill', 'Jackie-Marie', 'Starlight' and 'Kingfisher II'. Very sensible names they are too, almost predictable, This being in marked contrast to the fishermen themselves who bear names such as Nutty, Plugger, Tonks and Worm.

Cadgwith. Down the Hill

A stream flows beneath the road just here then reappears to divide the beach roughly in two. With all the rain it has carved itself a small canyon through the sand and pebbles down to meet the lacey green froth of tide. Gulls invariably congregate at this point to have a nice bath a fresh-water drink and a pleasant squabble. Sometimes following stormy weather the cove is the temporary resting place of a lone seal, a great big whiskery chap who with his head well out of the water studies us mere mortals with as much careful attention as we pay to him, but he's not here today... Having surveyed the cove I'm ready for breakfast so up past the pub and out of the cove and up the hill. A cottage door creaks open as I pass and old 'Rene Jane's white head pokes out and KYE her little dog rather reluctant to sample this fresh morning air. Polite greetings are exchanged and I plod on upwards. Timmy's cat has been let in, that's good.

I take the 'short cut' up the rough path which in Summer is home to two dozen species of butterfly sundry lurking snakes and magnificent giant green grasshoppers; through Martin's cabbage field and over the third

stone stile. (slippery when wet) On my left appears the largest stack of crab pots I've ever seen, I stop and reckon there must be 600 at least, all neatly stored for Winter. Bigger patches of blue sky now and something singing up there that ought to be a skylark. A warm breeze rustles the palm tree by our garden gate and beneath it a single primrose provides its sunny promise of the coming Spring.

PUBLIC FOOTPATH

Up the Hill, Cadgwith

You can't get much fishier than Newlyn a fine harbour crowded with local and visiting fishing boats, a busy fish market, the merchants warehouses and all the nice clutter and gubbins to do with the business of catching, cleaning, packing and selling of fish. Nice shops too where the fish glutton can take his time selecting a little something for lunch.

PAGE No. 52

PRESSED PILCHARDS

FRESHLY CAUGHT CRAB SANDWICHES

VERY salty

VERY VERY SALTY

Pilchards pressed into service. In a wooden tub.
Newlyn Harbour

"Mullet Down yer Gullet" RECIPIE

The grey Mullet is just occasionally and all of a sudden marvellously abundant in the Cornish Seas, like the dainty Pilchard in days of old when a shoal is spotted it's "all hands to the net", for the fishermen and if fortune smiles on their endeavours great rejoicing, most particularly in the pub.

1 Mullet, the bigger the better. *
2 tbs Olive Oil (nothing fancy).
A 'Thumb' of Root Ginger, sliced not chopped.
1 Clove Garlic, chopped not sliced.
4 or 5 Spring Onions, chopped and sliced.
More Pepper than Salt.
Juice of ½ a Lemon.

Descale your fish with a blunt knife, tail to head outdoors on a piece of newspaper; if the scales are reluctant to become dislodged (as they often are) rinse very briefly under a warm tap and try again. Remove head, tail, guts and black interior lining, wash. Split nearly in half, open up. Oil your fish inside and out, lay on cooking foil in a baking dish, sprinkle everything else inside and wrap him up. Bake in a medium oven for 20 or 30 mins.

Serve with slices of nectarine and lots of watercress.

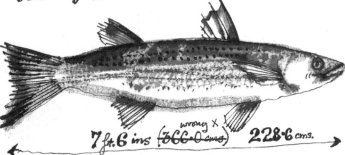

7 ft. 6 ins (366·0 cms) wrong X   228·6 cms.

* A Good Sized grey mullet.

He's joking

St. Michael's Mount, The Harbour.

It has been my pleasure and good fortune to sing "Away Down to Lamorna" on many a Friday night with our fishermen in the pub and I've been playing it on the sqeeze box for years but I had never actually been to the place, it was time to put things straight.

Like so many of the tiny coves around the Cornish coast this one is at the mouth of a short swiftly flowing little river that over the last few hundred million years has carved for itself a steep sided and beautiful valley or coomb.

A sunny day in early April is a perfect time to visit such places as the trees are not yet in leaf and so a great deal more can be seen of the river, rocks and general topography than in Summertime.

The valley was indeed lovely especially the cottages with freshly dug and planted kitchen gardens displaying the neat informality of vegetable rows pretending their plot of land is flat, level and free of boulders.

Lamorna Cove itself I found did not measure up to the romance and charm of it's famous song, interesting but not too special by West Cornwall standards.

So, on to Penberth. ▰▰▰→

This cove also has it's sparkling stream and wooded valley, I knew there would be no disappointment here as years ago I made an etching of it called 'Crabbers Retreat' for the National Trust. They being the owners of the place it was unlikely to have changed very much. Penberth is a small and remote but thriving fishing community with a dozen or so well looked after old style boats. Like Cadgwith it has no harbour so the constant hauling up and launching of boats is part of the daily routine, iron keels running in rusty grooves scored into the great granite blocks that pave the beach.

No fancy colours for the cottages just grey and white or white and grey with the occasional use of pale blue on window frames. Boats though can be as colourful as the 'skippers' imagination but here too shades of blue are favoured it seems. All very satisfactory.

The wether was just like Midsummer but by the banks of the crystal stream were bunches of violets, I put my money in the little box to take a bunch home for Wendy, a reminder that it was in fact only early Springtime.

Penberth

Manaccan.

It is a perfect Summer morning on the 3rd April. Having crossed bleak and beautiful heaths of Goonhilly and not been stopped by highwaymen I'm on my way to MANACCAN. I drop down a steep narrow lane and Suddenly the church appears Surrounded by a nicely arranged jumble of neat cottages. A church, a school, a village store; apart from peace and tranquillity what more could anyone ask? A pub of course and it's got one too.

St. ANTHONY, this church so history tells us was founded by Some grateful Normans storm driven here into Gillan Creek. The Church & a few cottages right at the waters edge, it's a simple and beautiful place. Since I last made a drawing here it has become decidedly YOTTY the Little beach being crammed with huge plastic craft. Unlike the photographer the artist can leave things out, so I have.

PAGE No. 57

St. Ives, Cornwall's most famous little town renowned the World over as a haunt of that curious creature the artist. From at least one hundred and fifty years ago this special place has been picked upon by such people, proper ladies and gentlemen too some of them were in those days so it was said.

Amongst those who chose to make it their workplace over the years have been some 'big names' and so St. Ives acquired the dubious distinction of being labelled an 'artists colony.'

Then they arrived in shoals as numerous as the pilchard and mackerel of the old days. You can't blame them St. Ives is a very nice place to call home.

Anyway, there have been plenty of excellent artists of various kinds who have worked here over the years and indeed there still are.

'One Man Show' St. Ives Quayside.

Todden Cottage, Cadgwith

PZ477

MARY ROSE

A fine little village is Coverack traditionally rivalling it's neighbours Cadgwith in the arts of catching crabs & lobsters and Mullion round the corner in smuggling. The rocky coast about these parts has accounted for more shipwrecks than you get winkles to a quart pot, sepia photographs of the broken ships together with salvaged artefacts cover the walls of the pub with accounts of the poor souls who drowned in the deep and of the more fortunate souls saved by Coverack's gallant lifeboat men.

The nice little harbour has hardly attered since I first painted here thirty years ago I'm pleased to report.

Even plastic "Tupperware" boats sometimes need to be repainted.

WINKLES DON'T

The Harbour, Coverack

Church Cove

Half a mile east of Lizard Town is the Church of L'ANDEWEDNACK the most Southerly in mainland Britain. It lies in a short wooded valley with a stream that tumbles into the sea at CHURCH COVE close by.

A pleasant lane wanders down beside the stream passing several thatched cottages and Vivien Bosustow's little sheds where he turns rough lumps of the local SERPENTINE rock into ornamental lighthouses, ashtrays and beautiful polished eggs.

Then the lane becomes a rough track and suddenly tiny but spectacular Church Cove presents itself, it still has a few working boats hauled up the steep natural slipway and the ancient pilchard cellars above, a reminder that not so long ago this was a busy *fishing* community.

Over the centuries pilchards came in their millions to Cornwall. From the cliff top the 'Huer' would direct the operations of netting, and bringing ashore the catch. Jesus did the same for his fisherman friends from the shore of Lake Galilee.

In the fish shop today despite a whole week of gales and rough seas are some lovely big red gurnards. Frequently dismissed as an 'ugly' fish (they're not of course just a little lugubrious) to us fish gluttons they are a true delight.

I couldn't help noticing that the fish shop lady looked my chosen gurnard in the face and quietly spoke to him as she placed him delicately on the scales, I felt forward enough to enquire of his name, she looked a little confusused.

"Bernard?" I suggested.

"Yes," she said, "Bernard the Gurnard, very good." — I'm easily pleased.

So low is the esteem in which the poor old gurnard has been held in in Cornwall that he is often used as bait in crab pots. A fact which to this land lubber seems a bit odd. Why sacrifice one certain tasty dinner in the hope that you might be lucky enough to catch another?"

However, more recently, thanks very much to television cooks of a fishy inclination a much wider variety are receiving the attention they deserve. Inevitably this will mean higher prices but as long as the fisherman gets a trully fair share that seems fine to me.

and me. WISE WINKLE

← limpet (very shy)

A Red Gurnard (*Aspitrigla cuculus*)

SIZE ⑥

Net Making, Sennen.

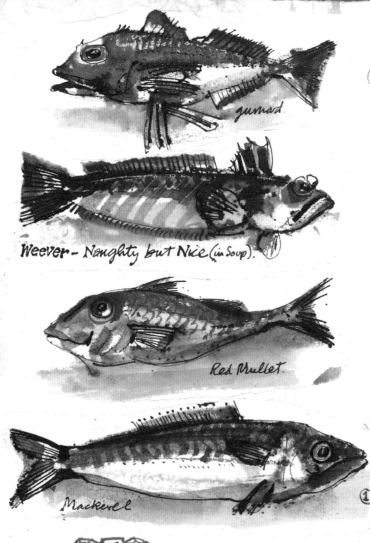

gurnard

Weever - *Naughty but Nice* (in soup).

Red Mullet.

Mackerel

PAGE No. 66

CHOUGH (chŭf) *n.* Bird (*Coracia Pyrrhocorax*) of the Crow family, (and what a delightful family they are) red legs and bill, usu. frequenting sea-cliffs. **CORNWALLS NATIONAL BIRD**

NO WONDER HE LOOKS SO WORRIED ①

① **Whether they ever made Chough Pasties in the establishment opposite I dont know. Nowadays Padstow certainly prefers fish.**

The Chough Bakery Padstow

BAIT BOX STEW
The Recipie (everything approx.)

3 lbs Gurnard, red or grey.
3 lbs Other fish, almost any except pet goldfish.
2 Big handfulls cleaned Mussels.
2 Large Onions. chopped
2 Bulbs Fennel. "
4 Sticks Celery, "
6 Cloves Garlic. "
1 Huge Old Potato "
1 Tin anchovies or 2 tbs Anchovy Essence.
½ tsp Chilli powder.
2 Lovely Oranges, cut into quaters.
2 Tins chopped Tomatoes.
1 Decent pinch of Saffron.
Almost too much freshly ground Black Pepper.
Water.   Half a cup good Olive Oil.
Herbs, 1 tbs dried mixed or 3 of fresh.
⅔ Bottle Red 'El Cheapo' Wine or priceless Vintage Claret.
Big bunch Parsley, chopped.

Obtain your fish fresh and whole, gut and wash them but throw nothing else away. Fillet your fish meticulously, hand rather than eye will tell you whether you have made a perfect job in removing all the bones. Chop fillets into soup spoon chunks.
Don't skin your gurnards.

Put head, bones and trimmings in saucepan cover with water and boil steadily for 30 mins.
Heat Olive Oil in large heavy pan add onions, fennel celery and garlic, stew gently.
Strain fishy water, add to stewpan with all other ingredients except fish chunks, mussels and half of the parsley.
Cook this for at least an hour, longer won't matter at all, you may need to add water, and give the occasional stir. Have a taste and add more of anything you fancy, don't overdo tasting or you'll spoil your appetite. Where's the rest of the bottle of wine?

Ten minutes before serving put some thick slices of proper white bread in a large baking dish, pour over some olive oil and dot with butter. Sprinkle with chopped garlic, herbs or arrange sliced cheese or tomatoes artistically on top. Place in a pre-heated oven. Put fish pieces and mussels in the pot. All will be cooked in but a few minutes.

Remove the soggy bits of orange, think about sucking a portion but don't. Remove the 4 or 5 bay leaves that I forgot to tell you to put in anyway.

Take the perfectly toasted breads and simmering stewpot to the table and modestly contend with the compliments of the gathering as they get the full aroma. Take the remaing parsley and toss high into the air making certain that some of it lands upon the surface of this most glorious of fish dishes. Serve.

Cadgwith from the Todden